T0162129

IF I DON'T
BREATHE

HOW DO
I SLEEP

IF I DON'T BREATHE

How Do I Sleep

JOE WENDEROTH

WAVE BOOKS

SEATTLE/NEW YORK

PUBLISHED BY WAVE BOOKS

WWW.WAVEPOETRY.COM

COPYRIGHT © 2014 BY JOE WENDEROTH

WAVE BOOKS TITLES ARE DISTRIBUTED TO THE TRADE BY

CONSORTIUM BOOK SALES AND DISTRIBUTION

PHONE: 800-283-3572 / SAN 631-760X

LIBRARY OF CONGRESS CATALOGING-IN-PUBLICATION DATA

WENDEROTH, JOE.

[POEMS. SELECTIONS]

IF I DON'T BREATHE HOW DO I SLEEP /

JOE WENDEROTH. — FIRST EDITION.

PAGES CM

ISBN 978-1-933517-88-9 — ISBN 978-1-933517-87-2

I. TITLE.

PS3573.E515A6 2014

811'.54—DC23

2013022980

DESIGNED AND COMPOSED BY QUEMADURA

PRINTED IN THE UNITED STATES OF AMERICA

9   8   7   6   5   4   3   2   1

FIRST EDITION

WAVE BOOKS 043

POEMS FROM THIS BOOK APPEARED PREVIOUSLY

IN *APR*, *BODY*, *COCONUT*, *FLOATING WOLF

QUARTERLY*, *GIGANTIC*, *GRANTA*, *HTMLGIANT*,

INSCRIPTIONS OF THE SEIZURE STATE,

TRIQUARTERLY, AND *YOUR IMPOSSIBLE VOICE*.

FOR ANN HUGHES

The Definition of Melody – is –
That Definition is none –

EMILY DICKINSON

IF I DON'T BREATHE

How Do I Sleep

SATAN IS REAL

I know

you know

how to sing

but who taught you

Notice first that your clown is made up almost entirely
of ligaments, cartilage, bursae, menisci.
Technically, a clown has only one bone—
the forehead—
and that is where your assembly must begin.
Put the forehead in place—
which is to say,
place the forehead on your kitchen table.
Feel the sadness of the clown's bowed head,
its willful eyeless despair.
The rest of the clown should come together easily
once this sadness has been felt.
As he begins to take shape, it will be noticed
that he is clinging desperately to the kitchen table.
This is absolutely normal.
Indeed, if it is not difficult to remove your clown
from the table on which it has been assembled,
you have probably done something wrong.
Probably a clown like that is going to disappoint someone.

—(If Only) the gentle bear of time
could swallow us (whole)
into a kind of cartoon silence

(a kind of crude and inadequate tourniquet

for the mind)—

I very recently came into complete possession of where I am.
I was like: *"oh ... I see ..."*
Trouble is:
having complete possession of where I am
diminishes the potential of my dramatic arc.
Learning, for instance, is no longer possible.
Discovery is no longer possible.
The changes that occur to the setting and the characters
are nothing but themselves.
It gets harder and harder for me to give a fuck.
I no longer *fear* the way those around me fear.
I can't see the danger that guides them,
and they can't see the danger that guides me.
It's a physical comedy.
The Professor.
I don't know what to say.

HUMMINGBIRD FEEDER

                    a *trap*
for what

you've seen and heard
but never noticed

          a trap
                                        (never mind
                                          this poem)
a festive artifact
to which
something is lured

before which

something
                    barely rests

feasting

HANGING UP SOME XMAS
LIGHTS IN LATE FEBRUARY

completely lost now

completely gone

those days we had

what were they for
where were they *from*

sometimes a few words together
are able to call out
to the dead

who are never present
and never reply

EARLY CAPITALISM

they are perfecting the pillow
with which
you are being suffocated

now it sings to you
and shows you pictures

Imagine a high-rise Casino that,
instead of rising up into the air,
      descends into the earth,
   a massive elegant mineshaft.
Each floor has the same appearance:
lush red carpet and pristine green gaming tables
surrounded by row upon row of flashing
and forever gently dinging slot machines.
Every inch of every floor
imbued with exactly the same amount of light,
which is substantial, and completely artificial.

With one exception.
      The first floor is built upon the surface of the earth,
      and so,
rises up some twenty feet into the light of the sun.
There are no windows, but there is a door.
How else could anyone get in?
There always has to be a door.

And when someone opens that door,
the light of day FLOODS IN.
         And if someone is there to see the light of day

    FLOOD IN,
the Casino is suddenly and completely destroyed:
a hopeless and pathetic waste of time,
an addict and a dealer.

Best then to avoid the first floor.
Best to make your way down.
One floor down is enough, really,
to be safe,
but the farther down you go,
the safer you feel.
Imagine yourself eighty floors down.
Imagine the stability of the light,
that deep in the ground.

remains
are sifted

out of respect

special attention
is paid
to nothing

STUTTERER'S HOLIDAY SONG

drowning in the sound
of crowded glory

holes for police
men's wives

hummingbird meat
on the grille

screaming
on the air

where the
where the

sewers empty
of trances

completely
sometimes

and again
I submit

the resignation
of the masses

SINCERITY

We laid the puppet in his bed as usual,
his bed of dry bloody tissues.
We had just settled in to watch
the unsubsided remain
when the puppet began to cry
in a really cliché way,
his stupid wishes beyond description.
A syringe was called for.
The inside of the puppet was called for.
He tried to sleep and he just couldn't.
He tried to dream and he couldn't.
His efforts were sincere,
and made everyone love him.
The whole thing is rigged.

LANGUAGE

it eats me
sometimes

like thunder
eats the sleep
of mice

like almost forgotten faces
open up the true silence
of the tongue

THE FUTURE

let us celebrate
in every way
it does not
have us

NINE-PIECE FLAMELESS
GLITTER VILLAGE WITH TIMER

what are we
if not
unexpected

   (a sudden end
to mass)

sirens cutting
through the symphony

a dull forced path

a sameness to ride like a horse
made of fire and rising wind

EVENING WITHOUT NEWS

. . . the wolverine orchestra emerges
. . . the golden ceiling blackens

petty
timorous beasts
all sleep-aligned

all dumb and loud
with their sleep

look at them not coming
true

behold the soft implosion
of attention

in the small-town crowd
standing bored

all along
the little parade route

naming the floats
as they roll by

there's *The Blood-Soaked Gurney*
there's *The Virgin*

following close behind
later on

The Missing Body
will come by

The Missing Body
is always last

a sort of climactic event
after which

there is but
to eat

LIKE GRANDFATHER, FOR INSTANCE, OR
LIKE A POSSUM LIVING IN YOUR BACKYARD

At first you treat him as a nobility—
a miraculous figure(head)

with no real office.

Then he dies.

Then you see what's written on his hard drive.

Unforgivable things.

You miss him.

Discard demonstrations of bravery,
demonstrations of compassion,
intelligence, *style*.

Nobody cares.

Discard jokes.
Discard that tone.
That tone is chock-full of rotting jokes.
Let them rot.
Let them come closer and closer to inaudible—
closer and closer to a quiet rotten mass.

There you go.

THE DOCTOR'S ADVICE

stop everything
and wait

MANUFACTURING CONSENT

some things are expected of me
all syllabi must be sent to Secretary X
for instance
by such and such a date

and sometimes I forget to send

and I am gently reminded

and *still*   let's say   I do not send

then maybe there is one last request

and even then maybe I am too busy

well
there is a point where they give up asking
        a point where they consent to live on
with an imperfect archive

maybe we shouldn't talk about it

THE SACRIFICE

I go with friends sometimes over to Woodland
to Big Mac Daddy's authentic Irish pub
to get drunk and sing karaoke.
This last time, on St. Paddy's Day,
the karaoke guy's father had died
earlier in the day, and suddenly he tells us this,
and I thought at first that there would be a punch line,
but there wasn't. Just:
"in a plane crash."
And so then he sings a song to his dad—
that Clapton song about
when I see you in Heaven—
and a woman from somewhere in the bar
goes over to him and hugs him,
and he's singing and crying
while she hugs him.
Then the owner of the bar gets up there
and says how close the karaoke guy
was to his dad, and says
how it's a demonstration of character
that he came in to work tonite.

"I wouldn't have come in," he says.

"So let's support him," he says.

"He's a great guy."

We cheered.

There were twenty-five of us

in the dim bar, give or take.

Twenty-five souls.

We cheered.

We confessed to being *still alive*.

Without irony, we were suddenly able to believe

in the shapes shifting in the dim light—

we sang drank and danced.

But there was nothing we could do to support him.

HE STOPPED LOVING HER TODAY

APRIL 26, 2013

death crowds

its way
into song

too beautifully now

and for too many days

it is impossible
the refrain

I let the birds out of their cage

(let them sit on top of their cage, at least)

because tonite

everything is free.

EVERYTHING.

    God's love.

    An elephant.

    A baby dinosaur.

Free

One is able to engage room in one of two ways:
as a *read* surface,
or as the Yes-And-No Tunnel.
The Yes-And-No Tunnel is not really a tunnel.
It has no entrance and no exit.
It only gets wider in every direction.
Those born in the Yes-And-No Tunnel
(and there is nowhere else to be born)
are alive and dead at the same time.
This condition—*contradiction*—urges
them incessantly to learn
to read.
Every *read* surface is a brief dream-
collapsing
of the Yes-And-No Tunnel.
Every act of reading
is the violence
that that dream
takes.
Meaning destroys space
with a little jingle.
Every call could be the one.

WAY IN THE MIDDLE OF THE AIR

A PLAY IN ONE ACT

ACT ONE:

Stage Directions

Interior: five folding chairs around a cheap folding table, which has a shadeless lamp (40-watt bulb) and some magazines on it. The folding chairs are barely illuminated by the lamp, and the stage beyond the chairs is completely dark. Gusts of air are apparent from the very start, and they pick up steadily. After thirty seconds, a rustling of the magazines on the table becomes apparent, and THE VOICE begins to speak. THE VOICE is disembodied, and is that of a confident, middle-aged, white, lower-middle-class American woman (preferably from Baltimore—Dundalk, specifically). She speaks with some degree of amusement, and some degree of bitterness. THE VOICE is amplified so that it is audible above the gusts of air, even as they increase.

THE VOICE: Eat all the bacon and donuts you want. (*Two-second pause*) How could the doctor stop you. (*Four-second pause*) You've found that line—that gray area: *slow, pleasant suicide* . . .

The gusts of air escalate as THE VOICE *speaks. Soon after* THE VOICE *has finished speaking, the gusts become so great that they knock over the chairs and the table and the bulb of the lamp bursts on the floor. When the bulb of the lamp bursts—which is to say, roughly thirty seconds after* THE VOICE *has finished speaking—the gusts suddenly come to a complete stop. The stage—indeed, the whole theater—is sunk in unblemished, soundless darkness. These conditions—silent darkness—are maintained for five minutes, and then a curtain falls (invisibly), the lights of the theater come up, and the play is over.*

Air is not air.

Light is not light.

Taste buds are not taste buds.

Word-count is not word-count.

Angel of death is not angel of death.

Original habitat is not original habitat.

This is not to say that you are free.

This is just to say that you are unable

to remember your dreams.

You're my grandmother.
Your toe is on fire.
You're no longer able to read
except with a magnifying glass.
What you are able to recall . . .
    you repeat
with increasing concision.
Your hearing is almost completely gone.
You're almost there.

DARKNESS

I would have liked to have a small film crew (one camera) record my entire life. At the time of my death, in a celebratory gesture, this film would open in a local theater. It would play for years—indeed, for as many years as I myself lived. It would be the uncut and unedited footage from the one camera that was always there with me, capturing my likeness, my intention, my wavering attention.

Yes, let's go ahead and green-light this project. *Imagine.*

The film—*what to call it?*—premieres three days after my death. The time of my birth—9:30 p.m. let's say—is the start time of the first (and only) showing. Thus, for the entire length of the film, the time of day in the film is the same as the time of day outside. The theater itself—its darkened room—binds together the real and the imaginary, allowing the theater-goer to enter and depart the film seamlessly, as if my life were running somehow concurrent with his own. The day encountered in the film always dies in an imperfect (worsening) echo of the day from which it is watched.

The *stages* of my life are another matter altogether. Every the-ater-goer—in relation to my life—has a unique age, and a unique history of attendance. Some see me many times, over many years —some never see me at all. Some are not born until I'm on my deathbed.

The film would have quite a long run, one might say, trying to be hopeful. But really the film is not playing again and again—tri-umphant return after triumphant return—no, the film is simply *long. Overlong*, it might even be argued, considering its stub-bornly poor performance at the box office. It has to be admitted that there are often times when there is no one in the theater at all. In these times, the employees inevitably get to talking and fooling around behind the snack island. To arrive at the theater at this point is quite embarrassing. It makes the theater-goer *and* the film seem like a failure, a bad joke. A waste of significant power. But this is just a seeming—in truth, the success of the film cannot be determined by attendance. The success and/or failure of the film are always in the future, so long as the film continues to play. Best not to look to the future—best to look instead at what actually exists. A darkness. Repose. Moving pictures having to do with someone who is not there anymore. Moving pictures that no one has ever seen before... or will ever see again.

Buying your ticket at 3 a.m. when the film has been running for sixty years... you may think you know what you'll walk in on—

but you can never know for sure. Desire for quiet darkness—an old man asleep—might make you the only witness to open-heart surgery.

But do not fear. The darkness of the theater is *especially* restful when its star is torn open but lingering on. The theater would be packed, if every night of my life I had been torn open but lingering on.

HEART LIKE A GLASS MOUSETRAP

WRITTEN WITH DAVID BERMAN

Incarcerated fish take tight turns in their square ponds.
The boisterous obituary has always to eat.
The mind is jammed with images of battered seafood.

Sick children, dressed to the nines, come to mind.
Dark video burns crisscross their thin midsections.
Mother and father drink the bilgewater of the time it takes to cry out.

Each kid seems to occupy his or her own wayward ice floe.
The weather is total war because total war is called for.
The foundation is in thrash—revelations without gongs.

One sees fire where it's not supposed to be.
Mother and father have always to eat or to cry out.
I must have been crazy to think I'd ever regard a oneness.

the ordinary gory fitness of closed eyes
and a steadily beaten

heart

is not just one spell

LIKE A POOP SANDWICH IN HEAVEN

that the impossible *depends*
up on grammar

it cannot heal

is a fact

only ever
smeared in
to the sound
of laughter
and fucking
in the rooms
of the condemned

dream

structure

PORNOGRAPHIC APPEAL
(PRAYER) TO TEZCATLIPOCA

Agony is here.
>(Agony is there.)

Agony is where.
>(Agony is where.)

Agony is from *where*?
>(Agony is not from.)

Agony is not from where?
>(Agony is *wherever*.)

Agony is not like this.
>(Agony is not *like* anything.)

Agony is an infinity
of routes
toward nothing
at all—the open
lit routes,
unentered.
>(Unenterable.)

All
the intractable
distinctions.

      (The *you*,

the *I*,

      the *you and I*.)

Humpty Dumpty off to war.

      (The endless columns advancing.)

Touch us, Lord.

Take us before we're ready.

The weight of each troubled star is discussed.

Stars that believe in aliens.

Stars that secretly grieve the irregular movement of light.

Stars that destroy themselves by getting older.

Weight is always a problem.

It's hard to keep in shape.

ENTREPRENEUR

You ever notice how the month is always longer than the paycheck?
Well, I'm going to fix that. Get out your calendars and put a big
red circle around May 10th. That's the day you're going to get it
all back. On May 10th, I'm going to give you eight pieces of my
skull—handbattered, slowmarinated, ovenroasted bits of adult
male headbone—for *$4.99*. Can you believe that? $4.99 for eight
pieces of *my* skull? You would have to be *crazy*—*clinically* in-
sane—to turn that down. You would have to be some sort of
bizarre cartoon creature, unable to eat of the world you live in.

COVER LETTER

in my many years of service
to the organization
I have been the mysterious and muted current
of an open body

my face has been washed
with the blood of the true
afterbirth

I've been tampered with for ages

you need me

POLITICAL AFFILIATION

FOR DOROTHEA LASKY

I watch *Celebrity Rehab* and *Sober House* religiously,
high and alone.

But it isn't that.

That's not what I mean. No.
What I mean
is

I see *how*
such a beautiful person
can be gone.

It's not a learning experience.

It would be possible to have me watched. *I know that.* I don't know what it would really mean, though. What its significance might be. I suppose its significance for you would be one thing— its significance for me another. But could either possibly repay the mind-boggling expense that would certainly be incurred?

The only way I can justify the project is to imagine the vigilance of a detective whose work is so thorough it produces no significant results for anyone. He's my hero. His patience allows me to be myself.

EXPERIMENTAL POEM

where

was

the

event

going

to

be

held

_____

it doesn't say

..

..

..

that there are animals

[4 9]

GENETICS

My grandmother's nervous excitement
when I turn on my little video camera.
Eighty-eight years old,
"failing,"
and still she feels the need to perform.
Still she must audition for her part
in the stories the unsubsided will tell.
The stories aren't set in stone, apparently.
Even as we are.

FLOWERBOMB

the line of scrim (edge)

is writ in
by dust
carnage
hiber
nation

(not this)

WE SHARE ARROWS

FOR ALAN WILLIAMSON

My arrows mix with yours
in your quiver.
Your arrows mix with mine
in my quiver.
When we kill, it might be my arrow
or it might be yours.
It might have been me who shot.
It might have been you.
In any case, the animal will die.
The arrow is poison.
The animal will walk a ways off
and die.

THE ODYSSEY, BOOK I

You can talk with a bird, sort of.

Sing *at* one another, at least.

There are notes, series of notes,

that you both can recognize

and might repeat

or exchange.

It's just an acknowledgment of the other.

It conveys no dreams.

It's just a twisting of the air,

I know,

but it breeds a rugged affection.

And to have that sort of standing—

the sort of standing that allows you to seem

to *correspond* to what owns you—

this is not something

other animals can claim.

To meow, to bark—

this is not the display of a song.

Perhaps wolves.

People howl to wolves,

or in response to wolves' howling,

but only from afar,

and not as a human being howling to a wolf,

but as an imposter, a cunning mime.

This bird, on the other hand,

is right here in my living room,

making the same sounds out of the same air.

He dares to countenance his equality,

his capacity *to sing*.

The song we carry on

is here

between us.

It is quite literally

the same grave.

METONYMY

what moves

this poem

What I do is
I go down to the thrift store
and get a bunch of discarded action figures,
and I take them home
and dump them in my sink.
(The sink should be white—
pastels may cause overwhelming despair—
and there should be a mirror behind it.)
Then I take off my clothes,
close my eyes,
and masturbate onto the heap
of variously staring figures,
thinking of something else entirely.
When I come, I open my eyes,
looking myself in the eyes in the mirror.

I do not yet look down at the heap.

Before I consider the heap,
I run a straight razor across my forehead
ten times.

(This should always be done slowly—
or at any rate, should not be rushed.)
I hold my face above the sink,
my eyes looking still into my eyes,
and I let the blood drip down.
I let the blood drip down for ages.
My eyes looking into my eyes.
Then, when ages have passed,
I look down into the sink.
I look down into the sink
at the bloody come-splashed staring heap.
It's so beautiful!
Even so, I'm always glad to get back home.

AND SO, MY DISCIPLES

you are lost to me

a mass resurrection
intricately blinkered
and lumbering
into
you know
not where

Show business must not know something.

—the silence of solitary gambling is not enough

—the silence of solitary gambling is all there is

—all there is is not enough

—all there is is show business, silence

SNAIL

Hearted creature.

Life is always prey.

The *pulse* of the prey.

Minding the whorl of the shell,

I am just another predator,

deceived about the size and strength

of what I might consume.

Outside of this deception,

what could there be?

What you do is you take some dental floss
(well, wait—
first I should say that there is a mosquito on your leg,
and it is *biting* you)—
waxed or unwaxed, it doesn't matter—
and you gently *loop* the floss
around the mosquito's abdomen
(preferably between abdominal segment
one and abdominal segment
two).
Then you gently knot it—
and *gently* is really the key here—
if you make it too tight,
you may tear away the entire body
from the head and wings.
So be gentle,
and gently knot it . . .

and then *gently* . . .
gently . . .

pull . . .

If you are successful,
the mosquito will no longer be biting you,
and its stinger will not be lodged in your leg,
which means that your wound won't itch as much—
won't even *be* a wound, really.

Your success, however, leaves you with a problem.
You may not be able, that is, to *untie* the floss . . .
without hastening the mosquito's death.
And you can't just leave it on . . .
because what kind of life
could a mosquito cinched in floss
lead?
Would he even be able to fly?
The only way to really answer that question
is to take the floss-cinched mosquito
and go jump off a cliff.
If the mosquito is able to fly, *you will know*.

There is no farmer of the unsubsided.
You can't grow yourself.

There.

LETTER TO DICK CHENEY

I remember
as a child
thinking about torture
(and I've understood since then that torture is just

a clarification
of reality),

and I remember proposing
(to myself
alone)
the limited susceptibility of a nerve
to abuse
(the diminishing capacity of a nerve
to feel pain)
as proof
of some basic mercy
at the foundation of the universe.
Then, today, as I lay in bed,
my chest pressed to my daughter's back,
I hear (with my chest)

her heart beat—
how real it is,
and how separate—
how mercilessly separate.
And I think of you.

UNDERGRADUATE ORIENTATION

FOR CARMEN AND KITTY

To breathe is to *accelerate*
into a sharp curve.

It is not in your power to slow down.
It is not in your power to choose the road.

Your power
(if you'd like to call it a power)
is to choose the songs
between now
and the wreck.

In the house I have agreed to pay for
for the next thirty-seven years

there is a pantry—
with steps down into it, high shelves,
its own step stool—
an honest-to-god, old-fashioned pantry.
For this reason (among others)
I occasionally think of a cartoon mouse-hole.

That *purest* of thresholds.

That great impasse.

The difference between species.

The difference between life and death—
between homecoming
and the futility of desire.

The clean dark vault
as ordinary

in the imaginary house that holds it

as it is

unprecedented in reality.

The devourer debarred by scale:

genetic difference.

The devourer debarred by nothing:

an open door.

No wonder

he eventually disguises his mouth

to resemble it.

ALL OF IT GONE

FOR JASON MORPHEW

standing there about to piss
listening closely
(without effort)
to the play-by-play
coming from the other room

    then pissing
and hearing nothing but piss

the sound of the crowd
the mannered play
of gameward-looking voices
all of it
gone
all of it
no longer with me
(an echo of familiar voices
adrift in a crowd
that isn't there anymore)

the piss ends

of course

in time

and the sound of the crowd comes

slowly back

      (that sound—that sound

is a root crown

             a dumb clutching

at the darkness

of

all remembering)

it is always heavier than it was before

and always the majesty of the voices

it carries

in its gaudy crests

seems less native

to the one

it deafens

and keeps

from sleep

If you are a man . . . and you attend enough committee meetings
. . . you will be tempted to dress like a woman (assuming you don't
dress like a woman already). Every new meeting will tempt you
further, and before very long you will have to give in: you will
wear panties under your trousers. And you will sit there in the
meeting in your panties,
dazed, radiating
the uselessness
of your secret glamour,
as if the substance
and the procedure
of this terrible place
could be forgotten—
as if its blank barks of attention
could be unmoored
and set to drift
in gloomy quarantines
possessed
at least
of silence.

IDEA

call a book of poems

~~THAT THERE ARE ANIMALS~~

and *cover* the jacket like so:
~~THAT THERE ARE ANIMALS THAT THERE ARE ANI-~~
~~MALS THAT THERE ARE ANIMALS THAT THERE ARE~~
~~ANIMALS THAT THERE ARE ANIMALS THAT THERE~~
~~ARE ANIMALS THAT THERE ARE ANIMALS THAT~~
~~THERE ARE ANIMALS THAT THERE ARE ANIMALS~~
~~THAT THERE ARE ANIMALS THAT THERE ARE ANI-~~
~~MALS THAT THERE ARE ANIMALS THAT THERE ARE~~
~~ANIMALS THAT THERE ARE ANIMALS THAT THERE~~
~~ARE ANIMALS~~

—same deal on the back,
and on the spine, the title should be prominent,
once, in fire-engine red:

~~THAT THERE ARE ANIMALS~~

—and then inside the book,

all margins—all white space—

filled up,

like the cover,

so that a poem looks something like this:

~~THAT THERE ARE ANIMALS THAT THERE ARE ANI-~~
~~MALS THAT THERE ARE ANIMALS THAT THERE ARE~~
~~ANIMALS THAT THERE ARE ANIMALS THAT THERE~~
~~ARE A~~*Poem*~~THAT THERE ARE ANIMALS THAT THERE~~
~~ARE ANIMALS THAT THERE ARE ANIMALS THAT~~
~~THERE ARE ANIMALS THAT THERE ARE ANIMALS~~
~~THAT~~*it is just*~~THAT THERE ARE ANIMALS THAT THERE~~
~~ARE A~~*being*~~THERE ARE ANIMALS THERE ARE ANI-~~
~~MALS THAT THERE ARE ANIMALS THAT THERE ARE~~
~~ANIM~~*torn*~~THAT THERE ARE ANIMALS THAT THERE~~
~~ARE ANIMALS THAT THERE ARE ANIMALS THAT~~
~~THERE ARE ANIMALS THAT THERE ARE ANIMALS~~
~~THAT THERE ARE ANIMALS THAT THERE ARE ANI-~~
~~MALS THAT THERE ARE ANIMALS THAT THERE ARE~~
~~ANIMALS THAT THERE ARE ANIMALS THAT THERE~~
~~ARE ANIMALS THAT THERE ARE ANIMALS THAT~~
~~THERE ARE ANIMALS THAT THERE ARE ANIMALS~~

such that the book is a kind of enchanted forest—

such that each page of the book is a mesmerized ~~animal~~,

an ~~animal~~ patiently withstanding the knife of the poet,
who needs of this deleted world
to eat.

And the question was asked:
how could the limbless man
have *fallen*

from whose wicked breast
from what filth of a father

meat
eating
flowers
in dreams
are difficult
    to arrange

(an injured ship)
(blood to start the wind)

because they have nothing
to eat
    nothing but themselves
and the blood
to start the wind

NEMONTEMI

which kind of darkness
will it be today

sad to think about eating

sad to be anything other than a stone

or tongues cut out and given to the grass

tongues cut out and offered *as a gift* to the grass

in which there are no stones

lush grass with tongues in it

but no teeth

no lungs

no eyelids lifted up

    raised up and *held up*

                          it isn't clear

for what

THE DIFFERENCE BETWEEN
THE LIVING AND THE DEAD

I record voices.
People talking to one another,
sometimes to themselves.
I keep the recordings.
Years and years of recordings.
At night, before I go to bed,
I listen in to the file, on shuffle.
Sometimes I hear the voices of the living,
sometimes I hear the voices of the dead.
Sometimes the dead are speaking to the living,
sometimes the living are speaking to the dead.
They sound the same,
the living and the dead.
To tell them apart,
I have to listen less closely.
I have to remember what I know.

NOTES: *We Share Arrows*: The !Kung people of the Kalahari Desert live in small nomadic groups of twenty to fifty people—a handful of families. Their culture—a hunter-gatherer culture—is very old. In this culture, the hunting is done by the men, who use arrows that they have tipped with poison. Each arrow is "owned" by someone in the tribe—it may be a man, a woman, even a child. If an animal is shot, and can be found where it has fallen, its meat becomes property not of the hunter but of the owner of the arrow that killed it. It is this owner who decides the distribution of the meat to the rest of the group.